JAZZ, FUNK & FUSION

OVER 60 CLASSIC GROOVES
IN STANDARD NOTATION

Wise Publications
part of The Music Sales Group
London / New York / Paris / Sydney / Copenhagen / Berlin / Madrid / Hong Kong / Tokyo

Published by
Wise Publications
14-15 Berners Street, London W1T 3LJ, UK.

Exclusive Distributors:
Music Sales Limited
Distribution Centre, Newmarket Road, Bury St Edmunds, Suffolk IP33 3YB, UK.
Music Sales Pty Limited
20 Resolution Drive, Caringbah, NSW 2229, Australia.

Order No. AM1003024
ISBN: 978-1-84938-992-1
This book © Copyright 2011 Wise Publications, a division of Music Sales Limited.

Compiled and edited by Terry Silverlight and Felipe Orozco
Revised edition edited by Adrian Hopkins
Cover and Book Design by Fresh Lemon

Printed in the EU

CD recorded and mixed by Jonas Persson
Drums and additional music editing by Noam Lederman

CONTENTS

INTRODUCTION

Welcome to *Rhythm Guides: Jazz, Funk & Fusion.* This book is a reference guide for all drummers and rhythm enthusiasts. It provides easy and thorough access to the most popular and influential classic and contemporary jazz, funk and fusion grooves.

Strong knowledge of these rhythms will add to your resources and consequently broaden your knowledge of different styles.

This guide was made with the sole purpose of outlining the styles of the great jazz and fusion drummers that have contributed to, shaped, and, in many cases, changed the way jazz is performed.

The rhythms in this book are not transcriptions of actual performances and are meant to be used for educational purposes only. All rhythms presented here are interpretations derived from years of observation and performance by the editors.

HOW TO USE THIS BOOK

It is strongly recommended that you develop a practice regimen in which you devote some time to learn each style. Play each rhythm variation repeatedly until you can master the 'groove' of each one. Use a metronome and practise at several tempos until you are able to comfortably play each rhythm at any tempo.

Format
Each groove is presented in standard drumset notation. Most grooves are presented in two-bar phrases with repeats; there are two fills per groove. The sections on rudiments and brush styles will further your understanding and enjoyment of jazz, funk and fusion drumming. Enjoy!

Notation Key
Drumset

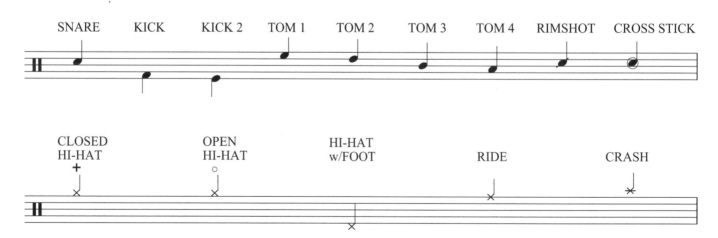

EARLY JAZZ

Big Sid Catlett

'Big Sid' Catlett came to prominence in New York City in the early thirties playing with big bands, and continued to be one of the busiest drummers for small groups until the early fifties. Although he had a fine technique, Catlett chose to play behind Benny Goodman, Teddy Wilson, Louis Armstrong, and all the other great soloists of his time in an effort to get the music to swing. He was musically flexible and played comfortably with early big bands such as McKinney's Cotton Pickers, pre-modern Louis Armstrong, and the bebop of Charlie Parker and Dizzy Gillespie. Fiery rimshots were one of his identifiable features, as was his style of playing time on the hi-hat with sticks instead of on the ride cymbal and snare with brushes.

Groove 1

(Groove 1)

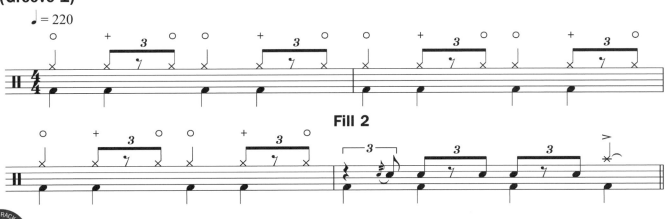

Groove 2

EARLY JAZZ

Chick Webb

Chick Webb was perhaps the most revered and influential drummer of the early big band era. He was a major influence on Buddy Rich and Louie Bellson, among others. Although he swung hard, Webb also showcased his technique and was one of the first to place the drummer in the spotlight as a featured soloist. Although he often played time on the hi-hat, he was one of the first to orchestrate band arrangements with rimshots and fills around the kit in soloist fashion.

Groove 1

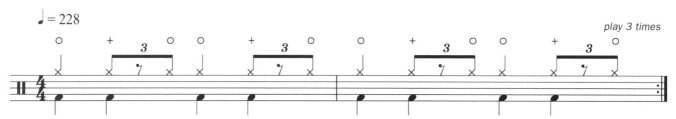

Fill 1

Groove 2

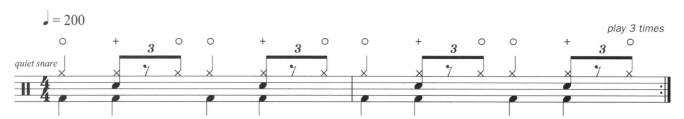

Fill 2

EARLY JAZZ

George Wettling

Considered one of Dixieland's greatest drummers, Wettling was one of the first to shift the timekeeping from the bass drum to the hi-hat and ride cymbal. He also had an ability to change patterns and colours behind each soloist, giving them their own spotlight and sound.

Groove 1

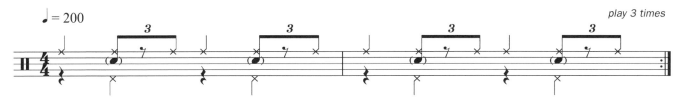

Fill 1

Groove 2

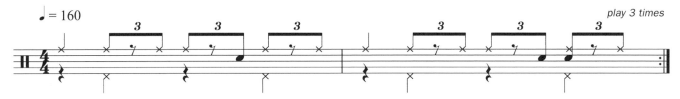

Fill 2

CLASSIC JAZZ

Papa Jo Jones

Jones was also one of the first to shift the timekeeping from the bass drum to the hi-hat and ride cymbal—particularly the hi-hat. He was the driving force behind the Count Basie Band. His focus on the hi-hat was a major influence on the drummers who followed him, and he would often take complete solos on the hi-hat alone.

Groove 1

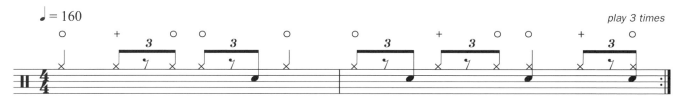

Fill 1

Groove 2

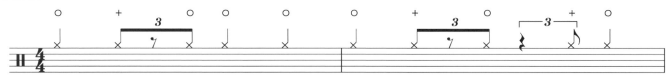

Fill 2

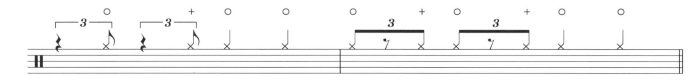

CLASSIC JAZZ

Kenny Clarke

Kenny Clarke helped define bebop drumming and further developed the shift of timekeeping from the bass drum and hi-hat to the ride cymbal. Where his predecessors played steady patterns on the bass drum and snare while playing time on the ride cymbal, Clarke freed up the bass drum and snare with more complex accents and patterns. He would often play 'bombs' behind soloists, earning him the nickname 'Klook.'

Groove 1 *(Feel is halfway between even 8ths and swing)*

Fill 1

Groove 2

Fill 2

CLASSIC JAZZ

Gene Krupa

Known for his snare press rolls and showmanship, Krupa recorded the first extended drum solo on 'Sing, Sing, Sing' with Benny Goodman. Along with Chick Webb, Krupa brought the drummer further out from the back line and into the limelight. He is generally recognized as the most famous drummer who ever lived.

Groove 1

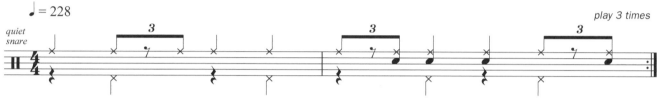

Fill 1

Groove 2

Fill 2

CLASSIC JAZZ

Max Roach

Max Roach internalized the drumming vocabulary that came before him and took it to a level that changed the sound and shape of drumming forever. He was the first to break up the steady ride pattern into countless variations and he developed the freedom of the snare and bass drum, being perhaps the first to recognize the hi-hat as an ornamentation of time rather than playing it consistently on two and four. Roach also further developed the drums as a melodic solo instrument and introduced possibilities that set a new standard in drumming. He achieved this over several decades—first as a sideman with Charlie Parker, Miles Davis, and Dizzy Gillespie, then as a band leader.

Groove 1

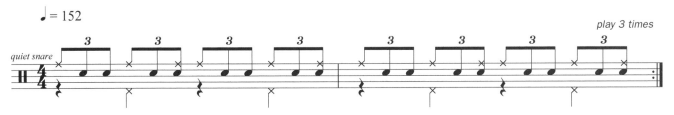

Fill 1

Groove 2

Fill 2

CLASSIC JAZZ

Buddy Rich

Although Rich appears on quintessential recordings with Charlie Parker and Dizzy Gillespie, it is for his influence as a big band drummer/leader that he's widely known. Aside from Gene Krupa, Rich is considered the most famous drummer. He further developed the groundwork laid down by Chick Webb and Gene Krupa as a showman and technician. He found new ways to orchestrate band arrangements around the drum kit with speed and four-way coordination.

Groove 1

Fill 1

Groove 2

Fill 2

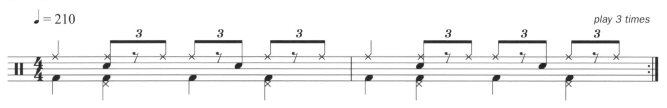

CLASSIC JAZZ

Jimmy Cobb

Cobb's greatest contribution is the deep groove and swing that he laid down behind many of the greatest jazz musicians. Rather than showcase the drummer as a soloist, his main focus was paving the way with the ride cymbal as the main groove, ornamented with tasteful bass drum and snare accents, resulting in a rich, warm sound from the kit.

Groove 1

Fill 1

Groove 2

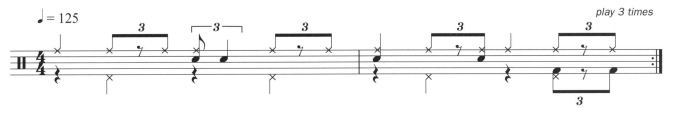

Fill 2

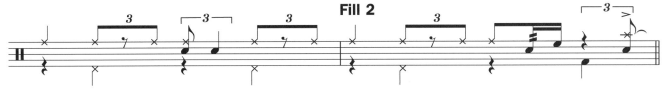

CLASSIC JAZZ

Ed Thigpen

Thigpen set the standard for jazz piano/bass/drums trio playing with Oscar Peterson and Ray Brown. His focus is keeping a swinging, steady groove. Due to the acoustic nature of this ensemble, Thigpen often leaned toward using brushes and consequently developed new vocabulary and techniques in that area.

Groove 1

Fill 1

Groove 2

Fill 2

MODERN JAZZ

Joe Morello

Morello's most famous recording is 'Take Five' with Dave Brubeck, where he takes one of the most recognized and featured drum solos in recorded history and put the drums further in the limelight. His use of space and sense of color and orchestration around the kit is a tasteful contribution to jazz drumming.

Groove 1

Fill 1

Groove 2

Fill 2

MODERN JAZZ

Elvin Jones

Elvin Jones had perhaps the most individual approach to jazz drumming of all. His use of triplets with his left hand is unique from any other drummer that came before him. The 'wall of sound' he created in his drum solos is difficult to decipher because of the personal way it is executed. One of the most identifiable aspects of his playing is the powerful, swinging groove he always created.

Groove 1

Fill 1

(Groove 1)

Fill 2

Groove 2

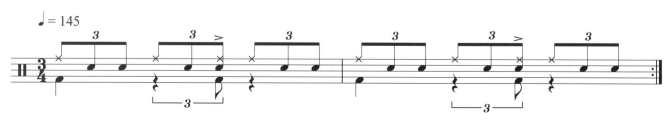

MODERN JAZZ

Roy Haynes

Roy Haynes' career spans six decades beginning with Charlie Parker and Miles Davis, then John Coltrane, Chick Corea, Pat Metheny, and, eventually, his own bands. Having roots in bebop, Haynes expanded that knowledge to modern drumming by finding new ways to accentuate time playing. He paved the way by changing the shape and patterns of ride cymbal timekeeping, augmenting it with more complex and independent accents with the bass drum and snare, and including the hi-hat as ornamentation rather than keeping time with it on two and four.

Groove 1

Fill 1

Groove 2

Fill 2

MODERN JAZZ

Tony Williams

Tony Williams changed the sound and approach of jazz drumming perhaps more than any other. He combined all the bebop elements that came before him with the more recent experimentations of Roy Haynes and others, and molded it all into adventurous, fiery and groundbreaking performances with the Miles Davis Quintet. Williams went on to further experiment with elements of rock and again changed the sound and approach of jazz drumming, being perhaps the first true fusion drummer. His use of polyrhythms, four-way coordination, playing the hi-hat on all quarter notes instead of two and four, and his development of playing hi-hat accents, has had—along with Elvin Jones—a major impact on modern jazz and fusion drumming.

Groove 1 (straight)

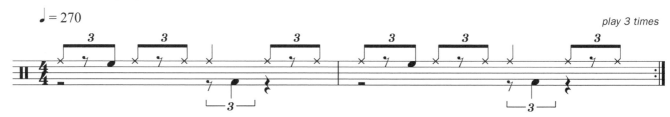

Fill 1

Groove 2 (straight)

MODERN JAZZ

Jack DeJohnette

Coming into prominence slightly after contemporary Tony Williams, DeJohnette, like Elvin Jones, has one of the most unique and individual approaches to drumming. His melding of bebop, Tony Williams, and Elvin Jones into his own personal sound has graced performances with Miles Davis, Jaco Pastorius, Betty Carter, and numerous others. Like Elvin Jones, his 'wall of sound' fills and solos are difficult to decipher because of their personal nature.

Groove 1

Groove 2

FUNK AND RHYTHM & BLUES

Al Jackson

Al Jackson is the driving force behind much of sixties and seventies soul music, having played with Booker T. & the M.G.s and on many of the Hi and Stax Records sessions. His style is deceptively simple, but his force and emphasis on the groove has not often been matched.

Groove

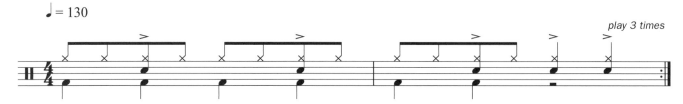

Fill 1

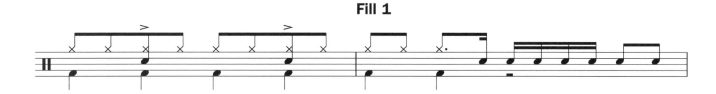

(Groove)

Fill 2

FUNK AND RHYTHM & BLUES

John 'Jabo' Starks

The drummer behind most of James Brown's recordings and live performances, Starks brought his background as a jazz drummer to funk. He interpreted the even-eighth quality of funk playing with a slight swing-triplet edge, placing the groove somewhere between even and swing. Changing the backbeat from the steady two and four to unorthodox, staggered placements was a major innovation of Starks'.

Groove 1

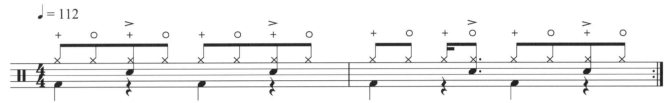

Groove 2

FUNK AND RHYTHM & BLUES

Clyde Stubblefield

Stubblefield joined John 'Jabo' Starks in James Brown's band, and together they created the quintessential 'bible' of funk drumming.

Groove 1

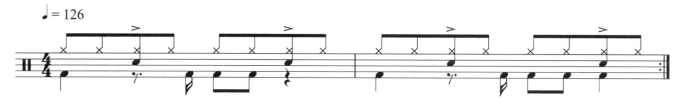

Groove 2

Fill

Groove 3

FUNK AND RHYTHM & BLUES

Bernard Purdie

Purdie is known for his great groove and funk backbeat. The drummer on countless hits and historic recordings for Aretha Franklin, among others, he tunes his snare tight and favours his rimshot backbeat over the silky time of his right hand—either on the hi-hat or ride. He created some signature grooves that lent themselves perfectly to the songs he was recording.

Groove 1

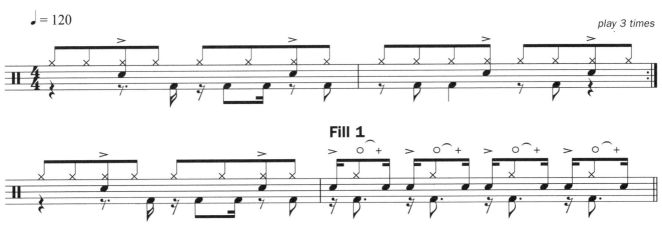

Fill 1

Groove 2

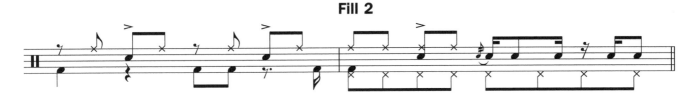

Fill 2

FUNK AND RHYTHM & BLUES

Harvey Mason

Best known for his unique funk groove on Herbie Hancock's 'Chameleon,' Mason has recorded and performed with a 'Who's Who' list of artists. Along with Tony Williams, he is one of the first to fuse swing with even-eighth feels, but in a funky Purdie/Stubblefield/Starks direction.

Groove 1

♩=112

play 3 times

Fill 1

Groove 2

♩=120

play 3 times

Fill 2

FUNK AND RHYTHM & BLUES

David Garibaldi

Garibaldi is known as one of the innovators of funk drumming through his work with Tower of Power. Like the modern jazz drummers that freed up the snare, hi-hat, and bass drum, instead of keeping straight time, Garibaldi created endless variations of snare drum, hi-hat, and bass drum placements and combinations with incredible independence, while maintaining a deep, funky groove.

Groove 1

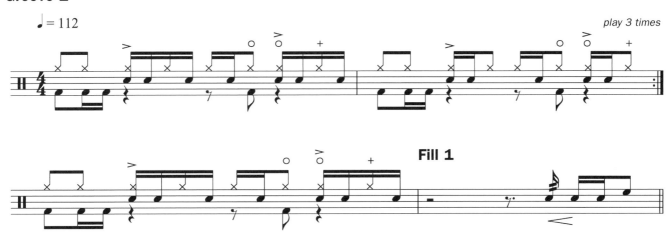

Fill 1

Groove 2

Fill 2

FUNK AND RHYTHM & BLUES

Mike Clark

Mike Clark, along with David Garibaldi, paved the way in funk music by experimenting with different combinations of hi-hat, bass drum, and snare placements in a funky setting. As the drummer after Harvey Mason in Herbie Hancock's Headhunters band, Clark incorporated the use of polyrhythms introduced by Tony Williams, becoming not only a funk innovator, but also an early proponent of fusion music.

Groove 1

Fill 1

Groove 2

Fill 2

FUSION

Airto Moreira

Moreira introduced a Brazilian percussionist's approach to drumming. As the percussionist in the original Weather Report band, Airto went on to play drum kit in Chick Corea's *Light as a Feather* band, then recorded several solo albums. His technique is somewhat unorthodox, and although he's an incredible timekeeper, his interpretation of fills and drum orchestration is undoubtedly derived from a percussionist's point of view. He is an early fusion pioneer with a different angle.

Groove 1

Groove 2

Fill 1

(Groove 2)

Fill 2

FUSION

Billy Cobham

Cobham, like Tony Williams, greatly changed the approach to drums while he was a member of John McLaughlin's Mahavishnu Orchestra. He combined in an innovative way the use of the double kick drum setup of earlier drummers such as Cozy Cole, Louie Bellson and Ed Shaughnessy, and the polyrhythms of Tony Williams, in addition to rock, jazz and funk influences. The speed and power of his single-stroke roll orchestrated over his multiple-tom setup is unparalleled.

Groove 1

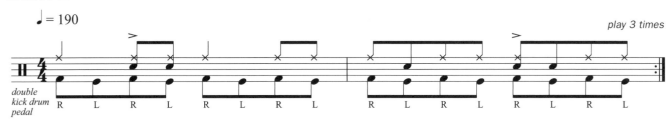

Fill 1

(Groove 1)

Fill 2

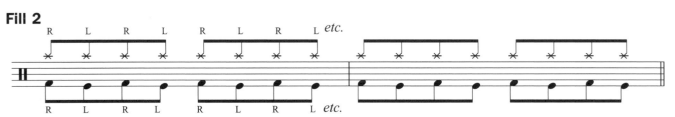

Groove 2

FUSION

Terry Silverlight

Silverlight is one of fusion's early pioneers, having played on the 1971 Barry Miles album *White Heat* along with Pat Martino, Lew Tabackin and John Abercrombie. The album is considered a turning point in the progress of jazz and inspired many of today's foremost fusion artists, including Pat Metheny. Silverlight's melding of various influences in that period, such as Tony Williams, Max Roach, British pop music and classical music, naturally led him to become a successful studio musician playing on hit records in a variety of styles. He continued to develop his use of over-the-barline patterns and presented this concept in systematic fashion in his book, *The Featured Drummer,* published by Wise Publications (AM980232).

Groove 1

Fill 1

Groove 2

Fill 2

FUSION

Steve Gadd

Gadd was the first drummer since Tony Williams to impact drumming on an exceptionally high level, and remains unmatched to this day. He has an uncanny ability to mold his playing to any musical style and contribute the most complimentary drumming possible for each project, all while maintaining his own original sound. The grooves he's created are classic, and the virtuosic patterns and fills he's developed in the jazz, fusion and pop categories have influenced almost every drummer since.

Groove 1

Fill 1

Groove 2

Fill 2

FUSION

Rick Marotta

One of the busiest pop/funk drummers of the seventies, Marotta played the classic funk groove on Steely Dan's 'Peg' and many other hit recordings. Although his influences are Steve Gadd, Harvie Mason and other funk greats, his approach is simple, and the focus is on the importance and depth of a good groove, always contributing to an original performance.

Groove 1

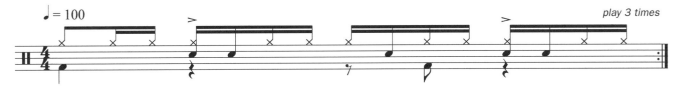

Fill 1

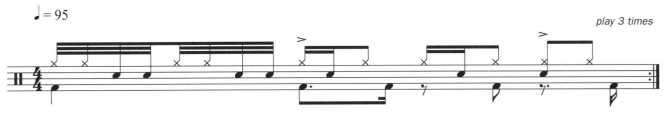

Groove 2

Fill 2

FUSION

Steve Jordan

A contemporary of Steve Gadd, Rick Marotta, and other studio session players of the seventies, Jordan's focus is on the funkiness and power of the groove. He possesses exceptional originality and commands an enviable technique, yet his ear for the groove has successfully linked his countless jazz, fusion, rock and funk recordings.

Groove 1

Groove 2

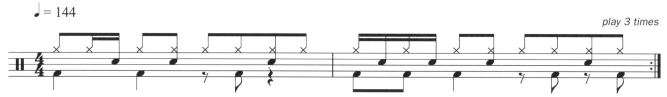

Fill 1

(Groove 2)

Fill 2

FUSION

Peter Erskine

Erskine has successfully packaged the influences of Steve Gadd, Jack DeJohnette and other drummers before him, by way of technical accuracy and execution. He has helped set the standard for current-day jazz/fusion drummers.

Groove 1

Fill 1

Groove 2

Fill 2

FUSION

Horacio Hernández

Hernández has brought to contemporary jazz/fusion drumming an element similar to what Airto Moreira brought three decades earlier. He has incorporated his Latin and percussion influences, thus creating a new approach to the drum kit. His ability to play the clave pattern with his left foot and coordinate intricate rhythms around the kit with precision is groundbreaking.

Groove 1

Fill 1

Groove 2

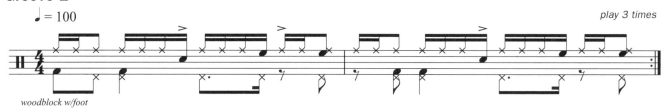

woodblock w/foot

Fill 2

FUSION

62 CD TRACK

Vinnie Colaiuta

Along with Peter Erskine, Colaiuta has set the standard for the contemporary jazz/fusion drummer. He has taken the best of the jazz/fusion pioneers and combined it into a pristine presentation. His diversity has placed him on countless recordings in the pop and rock fields as well.

Groove 1

♩ = 116   *play 3 times*

Fill 1

63 CD TRACK

Groove 2

♩ = 125   *play 4 times*

Fill 2

BRUSH PATTERNS

Many patterns have been developed for brushes. Here are five examples, to be played on the snare drum. Each of these patterns is in $\frac{4}{4}$ time, but they can be adjusted for other time signatures. Tempo is about 50 bpm except where indicated otherwise.

Soup

Place both brushes at twelve o'clock at the top of the head. Pressing both brushes into the drum head, start on beat 1 and circle the perimeter of the drum with the left brush counterclockwise and the right brush clockwise, finishing with both brushes at twelve o'clock on beat 2. Repeat this for each quarter note.

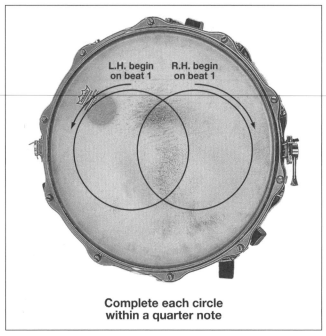

Complete each circle within a quarter note

Soup-Tap

Place both brushes at twelve o'clock at the top of the head. Pressing both brushes into the drumhead, start on beat 1 and circle half the diameter of the drum with the left brush counterclockwise and the right brush clockwise, ending by tapping both brushes at six o'clock on beat 2. Repeat this for beats 3 and 4.

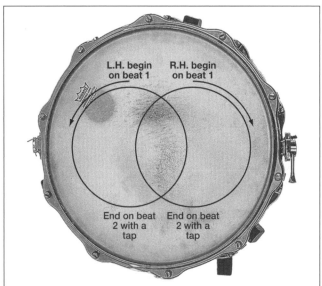

Half Moon

Beginning on beat 1, place the left brush at nine o'clock and the right brush at three o'clock. Drag the left brush clockwise ending on beat 2 at twelve o'clock and the right brush counter-clockwise ending on beat 2 at twelve o'clock. Repeat this motion for beats 3 and 4. As a variation, add taps with the right brush on the 'and' of 2 and the 'and' of 4 with a swing feel.

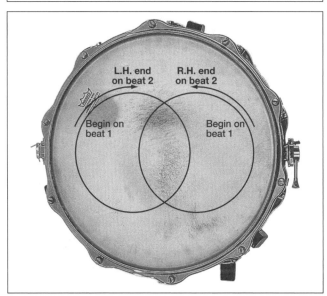

BRUSH PATTERNS

Circle and Tap

The left brush makes a smaller clockwise circle toward the center of the head starting at twelve o'clock on beat 1, completing the circle at twelve o'clock on beat 2. Repeat this for each quarter note. The right brush taps quarter notes toward the top of the head. As a variation, add taps with the right hand on the 'and' of 2 and the 'and' of 4 with a swing feel.

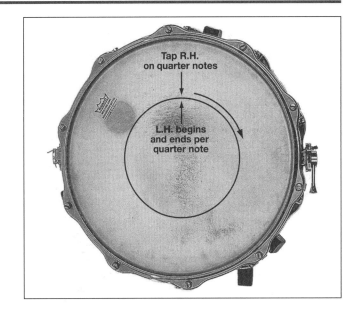

add (*) notes with r.h. taps

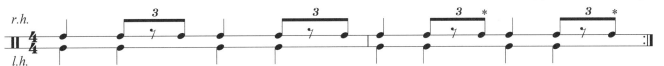

Samba Brush Groove

At the center of the head, swipe the left brush back and forth, with the downbeat quarter notes to the right and the upbeat eighth notes to the left. Accent beats 2 and 4. With the right hand toward the top of the head, tap a Latin bell pattern. Tempo can be 180 bpm or faster.

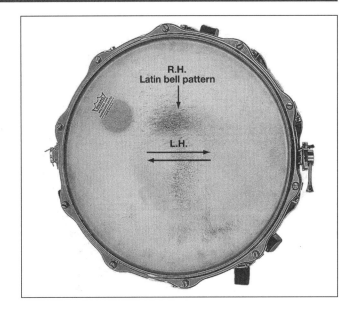

SELECTED DISCOGRAPHY

Big Sid Catlett

Armstrong, Louis. *The Complete RCA Victor Recordings* (RCA 63846)
—. *Louis Armstrong and His Orchestra, 1940-1942* (Classics 685)

Mike Clark

Hancock, Herbie. *Flood* (Sony 35439)
—. *Man-Child* (Sony International 9501)
—. *Thrust* (Sony International 86568)
The Headhunters. *Return of the Headhunters* (Verve Forecast 539028)
—. *Survival of the Fittest* (BMG International 140952)

Kenny Clarke

Clarke, Kenny. *Bohemia after Dark* (Savoy 107)
—. *Jazz Is Universal* (Atlantic 1401)
—. *Kenny Clarke in Paris, Vol. 1* (Disques Swing SW-8411)
—. *Klook's Clique* (Savoy 12083)
—. *The Quintessence* (Frémieax & Associés 235)

Jimmy Cobb

Cobb, Jimmy. *Cobb's Groove* (Milestone 9334)
Davis, Miles. *Kind of Blue* (Sony 1206)
Dorham, Kenny, and Cannonball Adderley. *Blue Spring* (Riverside/OJC 134)
Montgomery, Wes. *Full House* (Riverside/OJC OJCCD-106-2)

Billy Cobham

Benson, George. *White Rabbit* (Sony 64768)
Clarke, Stanley. *School Days* (Columbia 36975)
Cobham, Billy. *Crosswinds* (Wounded Bird 7300)
—. *Spectrum* (Atlantic 7268)
—. *Total Eclipse* (Wounded Bird 8121)
Hubbard, Freddie. *Sky Dive* (Columbia ZK-44171)
Mahavishnu Orchestra with John McLaughlin. *Birds of Fire* (Sony 66081)
—. *Inner Mounting Flame* (Sony 65523)
Sebesky, Don. *Giant Box* (Sony 40697)

Vinnie Colaiuta

Bona, Richard. *Tiki* (Decca 0007178)
Corea, Chick. *The Ultimate Adventure* (Stretch 9045)
Dion, Celine. *Let's Talk About Love* (550 Music 68861)
Sting. *Ten Summoner's Tales* (A&M 540070)

Jack DeJohnette

Brecker, Michael. *Tales from the Hudson* (Impulse! 191)
Corea, Chick. *Sundance* (Charly 150)
Davis, Miles. *Live-Evil* (Columbia/Legacy 65135)
DeJohnette, Jack. Extra Special Edition (Capitol 30494)
Kloss, Eric. *Consciousness!* (Prestige 7793)
Pastorius, Jaco. *Word of Mouth* (Warner Bros. 2-3535)

Peter Erskine

Elias, Eliane. *Brazilian Classics* (Blue Note 84337)
Steps Ahead. *Modern Times* (Elektra 60351-2)
Weather Report. *8:30* (Columbia 57665)
—. *Night Passage* (Columbia CK-36793)

Steve Gadd

Clarke, Stanley. *Journey to Love* (Epic EK-36974)
Corea, Chick. *The Leprechaun* (Polygram 519798)
DiMeola, Al. *Land of the Midnight Sun* (Columbia CK-34074)
Mangione, Chuck. *Together* (Mercury SRM 2 7501)
Simon, Paul. *Still Crazy after All These Years* (Warner Bros. 2-25591)
Steely Dan. *Aja* (Universal/MCA 10077)
Streisand, Barbara. *Guilty* (Sony 36750)

Dave Garibaldi

Tower of Power. *Back to Oakland* (Warner Bros. 2-2749)
—. *Bump City* (Warner Bros. 2616)
—. *East Bay Grease* (Rhino R2-71145)
—. *Urban Renewal* (Warner Bros. 2834)

Roy Haynes

Corea, Chick. *Now He Sings, Now He Sobs* (Blue Note 38265)

Horacio 'El Negro' Hernandez

Camilo, Michel. *Live at the Blue Note* (Telarc 83574)
—. *Thru My Eyes* (RMM 82067)
Hernandez, Horacio, and *Robby Ameen. Robby and Negro at the Third World War* (American Clave 1031)
Sanchez, David. *Street Scenes* (Columbia 67627)
Santana, Carlos. *Supernatural* (Arista 19080)

Al Jackson

Booker T. & the M.G.s. *Time Is Tight* (Stax 4424)
Franklin, Aretha. *30 Greatest Hits* (Atlantic 81668-2)
Green, Al. *Al Green's Greatest Hits* (DCC 1125)
Jackson, Al. *Atlantic Rhythm & Blues 1947-1974* [Box set] (Atlantic 82305-2)

Elvin Jones

Coltrane, John. *Live at Birdland* (Impulse! 198)
—. *Live at the Village Vanguard* (Impulse! 9005)
—. *A Love Supreme* (Impulse! 000061002)
—. *My Favorite Things* (Atlantic SD-1361-2)
Jones, Elvin. *Mr. Jones* (Blue Note BN A 110)
—. *On the Mountain* (Jazz Maniacs 5115)

Papa Jo Jones

Basie, Count. *Count Basie at Newport* (Verve 000161502)
—. *Count Basie: The Complete Decca Recordings* (GRD GRD-3-611)
Jones, Papa Jo. *The Essential Jo Jones* (Vanguard 101/2)
—. *The Main Man* (Pablo/OJC 869)
—. *Our Man Papa Jo!* (Denon 81757-7047-2)
—. *Smiles* (Black & Blue 975)

Steve Jordan

The Blues Brothers. *Made in America* (Atlantic 16025)
Fagen, Donald. *The Nightfly* (Warner Bros. 2-23696)
Spyro Gyra. *Carnaval* (MCA MCAD-1663)
Stern, Mike. *Upside Downside* (Atlantic 81656-2)
Young, Neil. *Landing on Water* (Geffen 490799)

Gene Krupa

Goodman, Benny. *Benny Goodman 1931-1933* (Classics 719)
—. *Benny Goodman and The Giants of Swing* (Decca GRD-609)
—. *Stompin' at the Savoy* (Bluebird/RCA 61067-2)
Hawkins, Coleman. *Coleman Hawkins 1929-1934* (Classics 587)
Waller, Fats. *Fats Waller and His Buddies* (Bluebird/RCA 61005-2)

Rick Marotta

Browne, Jackson. *The Very Best of Jackson Browne* (Rhino/Elektra 78091)
Garfunkel, Art. *Scissors Cut* (Columbia CK-37392)
Midler, Bette. *Bette Midler.* (Atlantic 82779)
Roxy Music. *Avalon.* (EMI 47438)
Scaggs, Boz. *Middle Man.* (Columbia/Legacy 65626)
Simon, Paul. *There Goes Rhymin' Simon* (WEA/Rhino 12413)
Steely Dan. *Gaucho* (Universal 93129)
Taylor, James. *The Best of James Taylor [2003]* (Warner Bros. 73837)

Harvey Mason

Benson, George. *Breezin'* (Warner Bros. 2-3111)
Brecker Brothers. *Brecker Brothers Collection Vol. 1* (Novus 3075)
—. *Brecker Brothers Collection Vol. 2* (Novus 3076)
Hancock, Herbie. *Head Hunters* (Sony International 651239)
King, Carole. *Fantasy* (Columbia 34962)
Laws, Hubert. *Best of Hubert Laws* (Columbia ZK-45479)
Mason, Harvey. *Ratamacue* (Atlantic 82904)
—. *With All My Heart* (RCA Victor/BMG/Bluebird 52741)
Ritenour, Lee. *Captain Fingers* (Epic EK-34426)
Turrentine, Stanley. *Best of Mr. T* (Fantasy FCD-7708-2)
Washington, Jr., Grover. *Mister Magic* (Motown 5175)

Airto Moreira

Corea, Chick. *Return to Forever* (Universal 30313)
Mitchell, Joni. *Don Juan's Reckless Daughter* (Asylum 2-701)
Moreira, Airto. *Fingers* (CTI 6028)
—. *Seeds on the Ground* (Sequel NEX129)
—. *Struck by Lightning* (Caroline 1607)
Shorter, Wayne. *Native Dancer* (Columbia/Legacy CK-46159)

Joe Morello

Brubeck, Dave. *All the Things We Are* (Collectables 7724)
—. *Time Out* (Sony International 65122)
Morello, Joe. *Another Step Forward* (Ovation 1402)
—. *Going Places* (Digital Music Products [DMP] 497)
—. *It's About Time* (RCA PM-2486)
—. *The Joe Morello Sextet* (Intro 608)

Bernard Purdie

Curtis, King. *King Curtis: Live at Fillmore West* (Koch International 8024)
Franklin, Aretha. *Aretha Franklin: Live at Fillmore West* (WEA 71526)
—. *Young, Gifted and Black* (Rhino 71527)
King, B.B. *Guess Who* (Beat Goes On 71)

Buddy Rich

Rich, Buddy. *Big Swing Face* (Blue Note 37989)
—. *The Buddy Rich Big Band: New One!* (Pacific Jazz 94507B)
—. *Buddy Rich and His Orchestra: This One's for Basie* (Verve 817788-2)
—. *Buddy Rich in London* (RCA 4666)
—. *Buddy Rich Swinging* (Norgran MGN-26)
—. *Mr. Drums* (Quintessence Jazz 25051)
—. *The Roar of '74* (LRC Ltd. 24103)

Max Roach

Roach, Max. *At Basin Street* (EmArcy 534391)
—. *Deeds, Not Words* (Riverside/OJC OJCCD-304-2)
—. *Jazz at Massey Hall* (JVV Victor 41561)
—. *Percussion Bitter Sweet* (Impulse! 122)

Terry Silverlight

Benson, George. *Twice the Love* (Warner Bros. 2-25705)
Change. *Miracles* (East West 6111)
Grant, Tom. *In My Wildest Dreams* (Verve/Forecast 849530-2)
—. *Move Closer* (Jive/Novus 1214)
Manhattan Jazz Orchestra. *Bach 2000* (Milestone 9312)
—. *Hey Duke!* (Milestone 9320)
Miles, Barry. *Fusion Is...* (Century CRDD 1070)
—. *Zoot Suit Stomp* (Unidisc 2024)
Nyro, Laura. *Mother's Spiritual* (Line 900924)
Parris, Gil. *Blue Thumb* (Okra-tone 4969)
Silverlight, Terry. *Terry Silverlight* (Cymekab 809)
—. *Wild!* (Artist One-Stop 42)
Simon, John. *Out on the Street* (Vanguard 79470)

John 'Jabo' Starks

Brown, James. *Dead on the Heavy Funk, 1975-1983* (Polydor 537901)
—. *Say It Loud—I'm Black and I'm Proud* (Polydor 841992)
—. *Star Time* (Polydor 849108)
Starks, John. *In the Jungle Groove* (Polydor 829624)

Clyde Stubblefield

B3 Bombers. *Live at the Green Mill CD.* (Alltribe Records 724)
Brown, James. *20 All Time Greatest Hits* (Polydor 511326)

Ed Thigpen

Thigpen, Ed. *Element of Swing* (Stunt 122)
—. *It's Entertainment* (Stunt 19816)
—. *Mr. Taste* (Justin Time 0043)
Oscar Peterson Trio. *Night Train* (Verve 521440)
—. *We Get Requests* (Polygram 521442)

Chick Webb

Webb, Chick. *Featuring Ella Fitzgerald* (Empire 836)
—. *Rhythm Man* (Hep 1023)
—. *Standing Tall* (Drive Archive 42427)
—. *Stompin' at the Savoy: 1934/1939* (Epm Musique 159722)
—. *Strictly Jive* (Hep 1063)

George Wettling

Teagarden, Jack. *Father of Jazz Trombone* (Avid 126)
Waller, Fats. *The Very Best of Fats Waller* (Collectors' Choice Music 141)
Wettling, George. *Dixieland in Hi-Fi* (Harmony HL-7080)
—. *George Wettling's Jazz Band* (Columbia C 6189)
—. *George Wettling's Jazz Trios* (Kapp K-1028)

Tony Williams

Davis, Miles. *Four and More* (Sony 1212)
—. *Miles Smiles* (Sony 1216)
—. *My Funny Valentine* (Sony 1211)
—. *Nefertiti* (Sony 1218)
Williams, Tony. *Believe It* (Columbia PC 33836)
—. *Emergency!* (Polydor 849068)
—. *The Joy of Flying* (Sony 65473)
—. *Lifetime* (Blue Note 99004)
—. *Wilderness* (Ark 21 810053)

CD TRACKLISTING

CD Track No:			CD Track No:		
1	Groove 1, Fill 1	**Big Sid Catlett**	33	Groove 1	**John 'Jabo' Starks**
2	Groove 1, Fill 2		34	Groove 2, Fill	
3	Groove 2				
			35	Groove 1, Fill	**Clyde Stubblefield**
4	Groove 1, Fill 1	**Chick Webb**	36	Groove 2, Fill	
5	Groove 2, Fill 2		37	Groove 3	
6	Groove 1, Fill 1	**George Wettling**	38	Groove 1, Fill 1	**Bernard Purdie**
7	Groove 2, Fill 2		39	Groove 2, Fill 2	
8	Groove 1, Fill 1	**Papa Jo Jones**	40	Groove 1, Fill 1	**Harvey Mason**
9	Groove 2, Fill 2		41	Groove 2, Fill 2	
10	Groove 1, Fill 1	**Kenny Clarke**	42	Groove 1, Fill 1	**David Garibaldi**
11	Groove 2, Fill 2		43	Groove 2, Fill 2	
12	Groove 1, Fill 1	**Gene Krupa**	44	Groove 1, Fill 1	**Mike Clark**
13	Groove 2, Fill 2		45	Groove 2, Fill 2	
14	Groove 1, Fill 1	**Max Roach**	46	Groove 1	**Airto Moreira**
15	Groove 2, Fill 2		47	Groove 2, Fill 1, (Groove 2), Fill 2	
16	Groove 1, Fill 1	**Buddy Rich**	48	Groove 1, Fill 1, (Groove 1), Fill 2	**Billy Cobham**
17	Groove 2, Fill 2		49	Groove 2	
18	Groove 1, Fill 1	**Jimmy Cobb**	50	Groove 1, Fill 1	**Terry Silverlight**
19	Groove 2, Fill 2		51	Groove 2, Fill 2	
20	Groove 1, Fill 1	**Ed Thigpen**	52	Groove 1, Fill 1	**Steve Gadd**
21	Groove 2, Fill 2		53	Groove 2, Fill 2	
22	Groove 1, Fill 1	**Joe Morello**	54	Groove 1, Fill 1	**Rick Marotta**
23	Groove 2, Fill 2		55	Groove 2, Fill 2	
24	Groove 1, Fill 1, (Groove 1), Fill 2	**Elvin Jones**	56	Groove 1	**Steve Jordan**
25	Groove 2		57	Groove 2, Fill 1, (Groove 2), Fill 2	
26	Groove 1, Fill 1	**Roy Haynes**	58	Groove 1, Fill 1	**Peter Erskine**
27	Groove 2, Fill 2		59	Groove 2, Fill 2	
28	Groove 1, Fill 1	**Tony Williams**	60	Groove 1, Fill 1	**Horacio Hernández**
29	Groove 2, Fill 2		61	Groove 2, Fill 2	
30	Groove 1, Fill 1	**Jack DeJohnette**	62	Groove 1, Fill 1	**Vinnie Colaiuta**
31	Groove 2, Fill 2		63	Groove 2, Fill 2	
32	Groove, Fill 1, (Groove), Fill 2	**Al Jackson**			

12345678